Editor
Lorin E. Klistoff, M.A.

Managing Editor
Karen Goldfluss, M.S. Ed.

Editor-in-Chief
Sharon Coan, M.S. Ed.

Cover Artist
Barb Lorseyedi

Illustrator
Howard Chaney

Art Coordinator
Kevin Barnes

Art Director
CJae Froshay

Imaging
Rosa C. See

Product Manager
Phil Garcia

Publishers
Rachelle Cracchiolo, M.S. Ed.
Mary Dupuy Smith, M.S. Ed.

Practice Makes Perfect

Map Skills

GRADE 1

Author

Mary Rosenberg

Teacher Created Materials, Inc.
6421 Industry Way
Westminster, CA 92683
www.teachercreated.com

ISBN-0-7439-3726-0

©2003 Teacher Created Materials, Inc.
Reprinted, 2003
Made in U.S.A.

Table of Contents

Introduction

The old adage "practice makes perfect" can really hold true for your child and his or her education. The more practice and exposure your child has with concepts being taught in school, the more success he or she is likely to find. For many parents, knowing how to help your child can be frustrating because the resources may not be readily available. As a parent it is also difficult to know where to focus your efforts so that the extra practice your child receives at home supports what he or she is learning in school.

This book has been designed to help parents and teachers reinforce basic skills with children. *Practice Makes Perfect* reviews basic skills. The focus in this book is a review of map skills for children in grade 1. While it would be impossible to include all map concepts taught in grade 1 in this book, the following basic objectives are reinforced through practice exercises (refer to the Table of Contents for specific objectives of each practice page):

- measure distances
- use coordinate points
- work with numbers
- follow and give directions
- develop a sense of direction

- use positional words to describe location or position
- use ordinals to describe location or position
- develop the ability to read a legend (or key) for information and to transfer this information to the map

There are 36 practice pages. (*Note:* Have children show all work when computation is necessary to solve a problem. For multiple choice responses on practice pages, children can fill in the letter choice or circle the answer.) Following the practice pages are six test practices. These provide children with multiple-choice tests to help prepare them for standardized tests administered in schools. As your child completes each test, he or she can fill in the correct bubbles on the optional answer sheet provided on page 46. To correct the test pages and the practice pages in this book, use the answer key provided on pages 47 and 48.

How to Make the Most of This Book

Here are some useful ideas for optimizing the practice pages in this book:

- Set aside a specific place in your home to work on the practice pages. Keep it neat and tidy with materials on hand.
- Set up a certain time of day to work on the practice pages. This will establish consistency. Look for times in your day or week that are less hectic and more conducive to practicing skills.
- Keep all practice sessions with your child positive and constructive. If the mood becomes tense or you and your child are frustrated, set the book aside and look for another time to practice with your child.
- Help with instructions if necessary. If your child is having difficulty understanding what to do or how to get started, work through the first problem together.
- Review the work your child has done. This serves as reinforcement and provides further practice.
- Allow your child to use whatever writing instruments he or she prefers. For example, colored pencils can add variety and pleasure to drill work.
- Pay attention to the areas in which your child has the most difficulty. Provide extra guidance and exercises in those areas. Allowing children to use drawings and manipulatives, such as coins, tiles, game markers, or flash cards, can help them grasp difficult concepts more easily.
- Look for ways to make real-life applications to the skills being reinforced.

Up or Down?

Draw a line matching each sentence to its picture.

1. Jan is climbing <u>up the slide</u>.

2. Hector is climbing <u>down the tree</u>.

3. Angela is going <u>up the stairs</u>.

4. Frank is climbing <u>down the ladder</u>.

5. Myron is going <u>down the slide</u>.

6. Isadora is climbing <u>up the ladder</u>.

7. Darren is going <u>down the stairs</u>.

8. Gabriella is climbing <u>up the tree</u>.

A.

B.

C.

D.

E.

F.

G.

H.

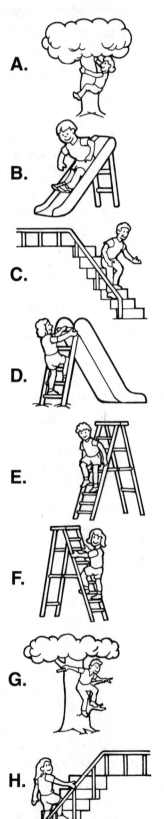

Up and Down

Write the word **up** or **down** to complete each sentence.

1. The ⬥ is _____ in the sky.

2. The 🐢 is _____ on the ground.

3. The 🐦 is _____ on the fence.

4. The 🐜 is _____ in the tree.

5. The 🐛 is _____ in the grass.

Left and Right

Trace the words.

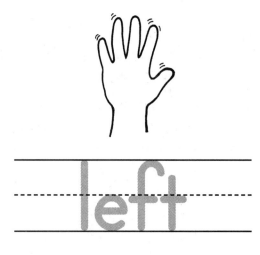

left

right

Which way is each animal looking? Write **left** or **right** on the lines.

1.

_____

- - - - - - - - - - -

_____

2.

_____

- - - - - - - - - - -

_____

3.

_____

- - - - - - - - - - -

_____

4.

_____

- - - - - - - - - - -

_____

Where Is It?

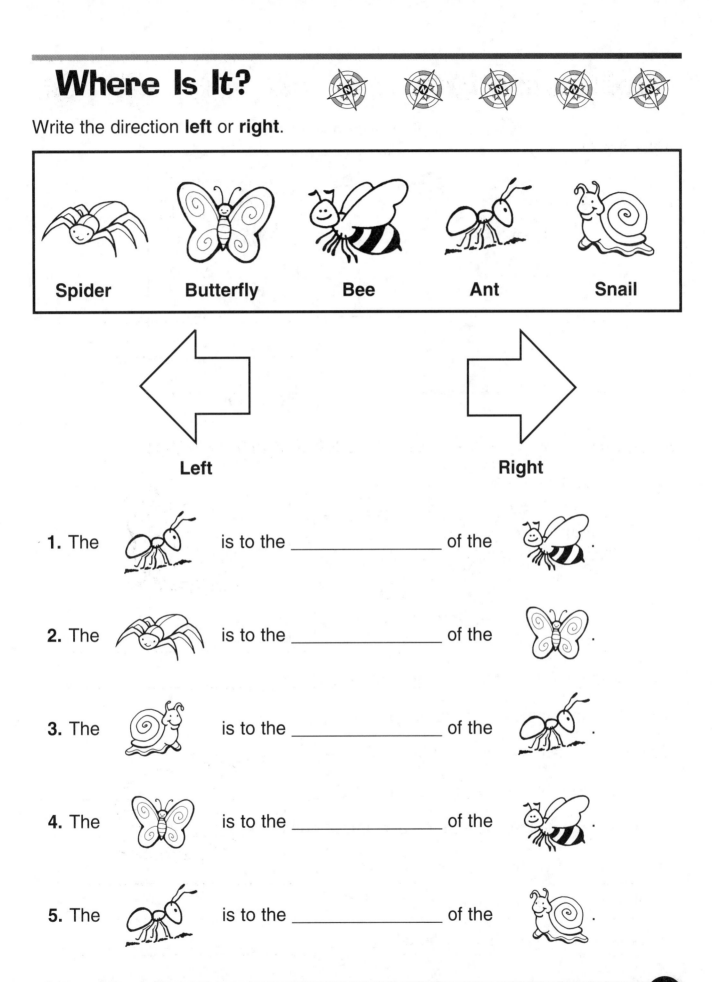

Write the direction **left** or **right**.

| Spider | Butterfly | Bee | Ant | Snail |

Left   **Right**

1. The ant is to the _____ of the bee .

2. The spider is to the _____ of the butterfly .

3. The snail is to the _____ of the ant .

4. The butterfly is to the _____ of the bee .

5. The ant is to the _____ of the snail .

Answer the questions about the Ritz Apartments below.

1. How many floors are in the apartment building? _____

2. How many apartments are there in all? _____

3. Which floor has the most apartments? _____

4. Which floor has the fewest apartments? _____

5. How many children live in the apartment building? _____

6. On which floor does the doctor live? _____

7. How many people live on the third floor? _____

8. Which family likes hamburgers? _____

Tower Living

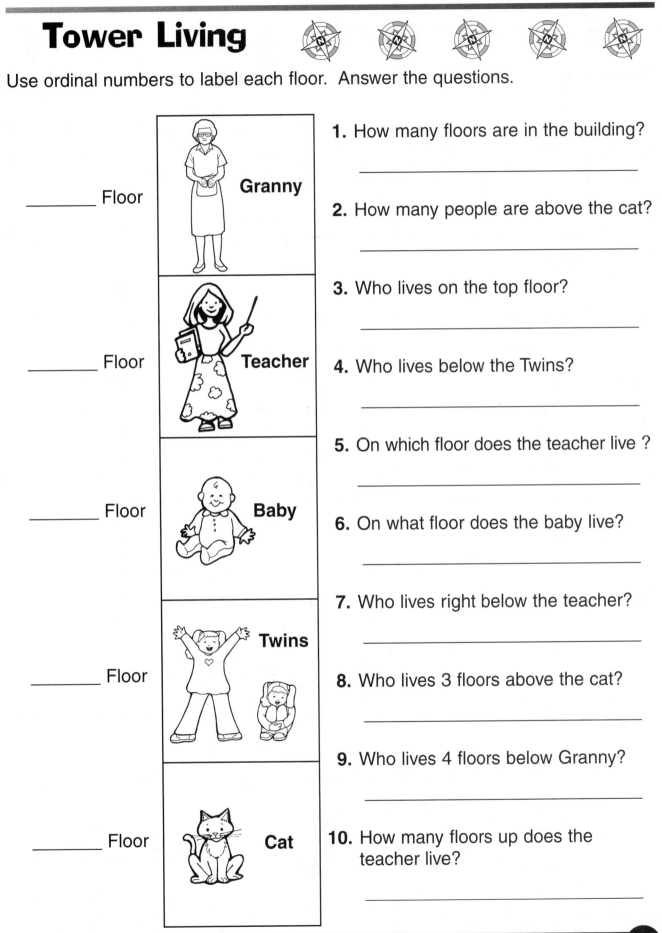

Use ordinal numbers to label each floor. Answer the questions.

_____ Floor — Granny

_____ Floor — Teacher

_____ Floor — Baby

_____ Floor — Twins

_____ Floor — Cat

1. How many floors are in the building?

_____

2. How many people are above the cat?

_____

3. Who lives on the top floor?

_____

4. Who lives below the Twins?

_____

5. On which floor does the teacher live ?

_____

6. On what floor does the baby live?

_____

7. Who lives right below the teacher?

_____

8. Who lives 3 floors above the cat?

_____

9. Who lives 4 floors below Granny?

_____

10. How many floors up does the teacher live?

_____

How to Get There

1st	**2nd**	**3rd**	**4th**	**3rd**	**2nd**	**1st**

Circle the answer.

1. 3rd from the right

2. 2nd from the left

3. 1st from the left

4. 2nd from the right

5. 3rd from the left

6. 1st from the right

7. Circle the picture that is 4th from the left and 4th from the right.

#3726 Practice Makes Perfect: Map Skills

Where Do They Live?

Write the directions to get to each person's house. The first one has been done for you.

1. 2nd on the right

2. ____ on the ____

3. ____ on the ____

4. ____ on the ____

5. ____ on the ____

6. ____ on the ____

7. ____ on the ____

8. ____ on the ____

Draw It!

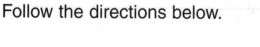

Follow the directions below.

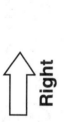
Right

Left

1. Draw a heart <u>next</u> to the gift.

2. Draw a star <u>above</u> the boy.

3. Draw a circle <u>behind</u> the mouse.

4. Draw a square <u>in front of</u> the dog.

5. Draw a triangle to the <u>left</u> of the girl.

Inside and Outside

Circle **inside** or **outside** to complete each sentence.

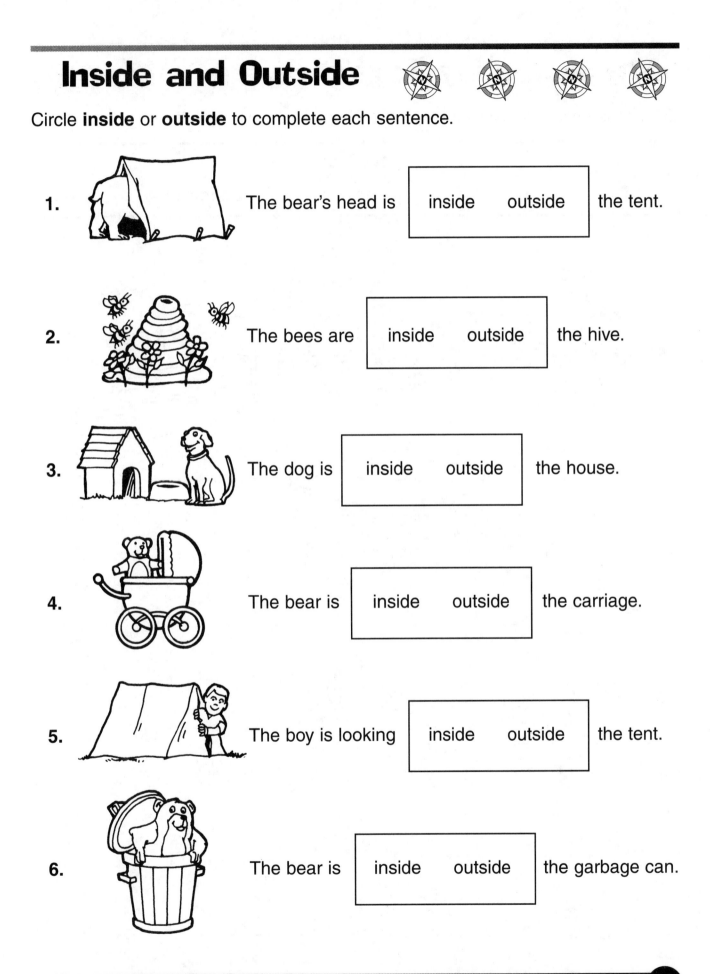

1. The bear's head is | inside   outside | the tent.

2. The bees are | inside   outside | the hive.

3. The dog is | inside   outside | the house.

4. The bear is | inside   outside | the carriage.

5. The boy is looking | inside   outside | the tent.

6. The bear is | inside   outside | the garbage can.

Use the words in the Word Bank to tell where each toy was left.

Word Bank				
behind	in front of	next to	on top of	under

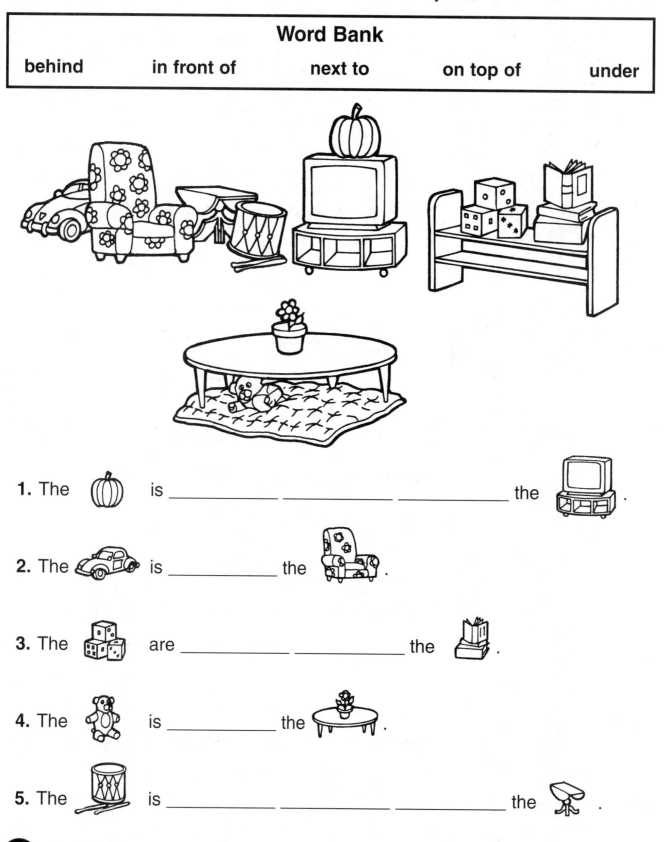

1. The 🎃 is _____ _____ _____ the 📺 .

2. The 🚗 is _____ the 🪑 .

3. The 🎲 are _____ _____ the 📖 .

4. The 🧸 is _____ the 🌼 .

5. The 🥁 is _____ _____ _____ the 🪑 .

In a Line

Use the phrases in the Word Bank to complete each sentence. Each phrase can be used only one time.

Word Bank

the left of	between	next to	beside	the right of
←				→

1. ___ is _____ _____ ___ .

2. ___ is _____ ___ and ___ .

3. ___ is to _____ _____ _____ ___ .

4. ___ is to _____ _____ ___ .

5. ___ is _____ ___ .

Everything in Its Place

Use the words in the Word Bank to complete each sentence. Each word is used only one time.

Word Bank					
above	below	down	over	under	up

1. The cat is _____ in the tree.

2. The bird is _____ the cat.

3. The dog is _____ the tree.

4. The sign is _____ the dog.

5. The dragonfly is _____ the fire hydrant.

6. The dog is sitting _____ on the ground.

The Schoolhouse

Use the word(s) in the Word Bank to complete each sentence. The words are only used one time.

Word Bank				
behind	under	in front of	inside	next to
on	on top of	outside	right of	

1. The bell is _____ _____ _____ the roof.

2. The bus is _____ the road.

3. The school is _____ the bus.

4. The teacher is _____ _____ _____ the school.

5. The road is _____ the bus.

6. The bus driver is _____ the bus.

7. The boy with the hat is to the _____ _____ the girl.

8. The dog is _____ _____ the girl.

9. The dog is _____ the bus.

Sports Shop

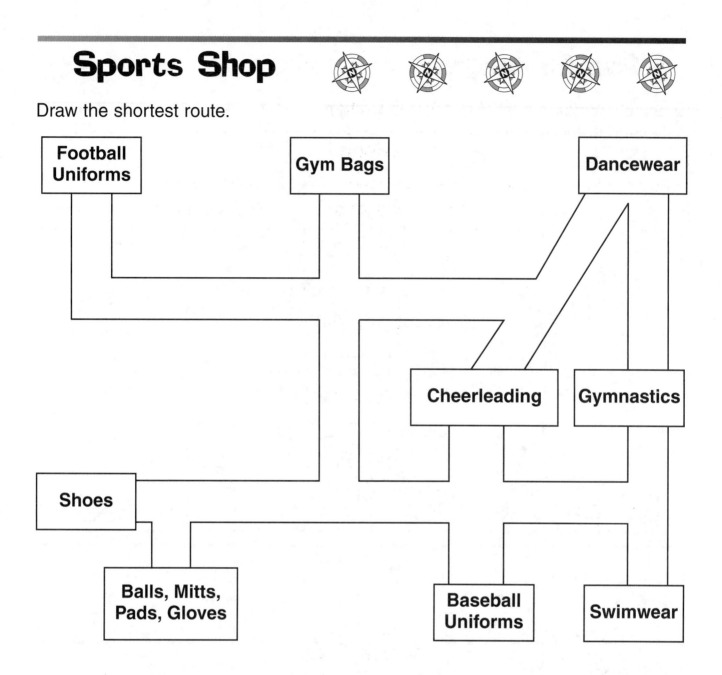

Draw the shortest route.

1. Use a red crayon to draw the route from Shoes to Gymnastics.

2. Use an orange crayon to draw the route from Dancewear to Cheerleading.

3. Use a yellow crayon to draw the route from Balls, Mitts, Pads, Gloves to Swimwear.

4. Use a green crayon to draw the route from Football Uniforms to Baseball Uniforms.

5. Use a blue crayon to draw the route from Gymnastics to Baseball Uniforms.

6. Use a purple crayon to draw the route from Gym Bags to Shoes.

Coloring Maps

Color the map below as shown in the legend.

Legend

Pools = blue	Trees = green	Parks = brown
Houses = purple	Stores = orange	Roads and Streets = red

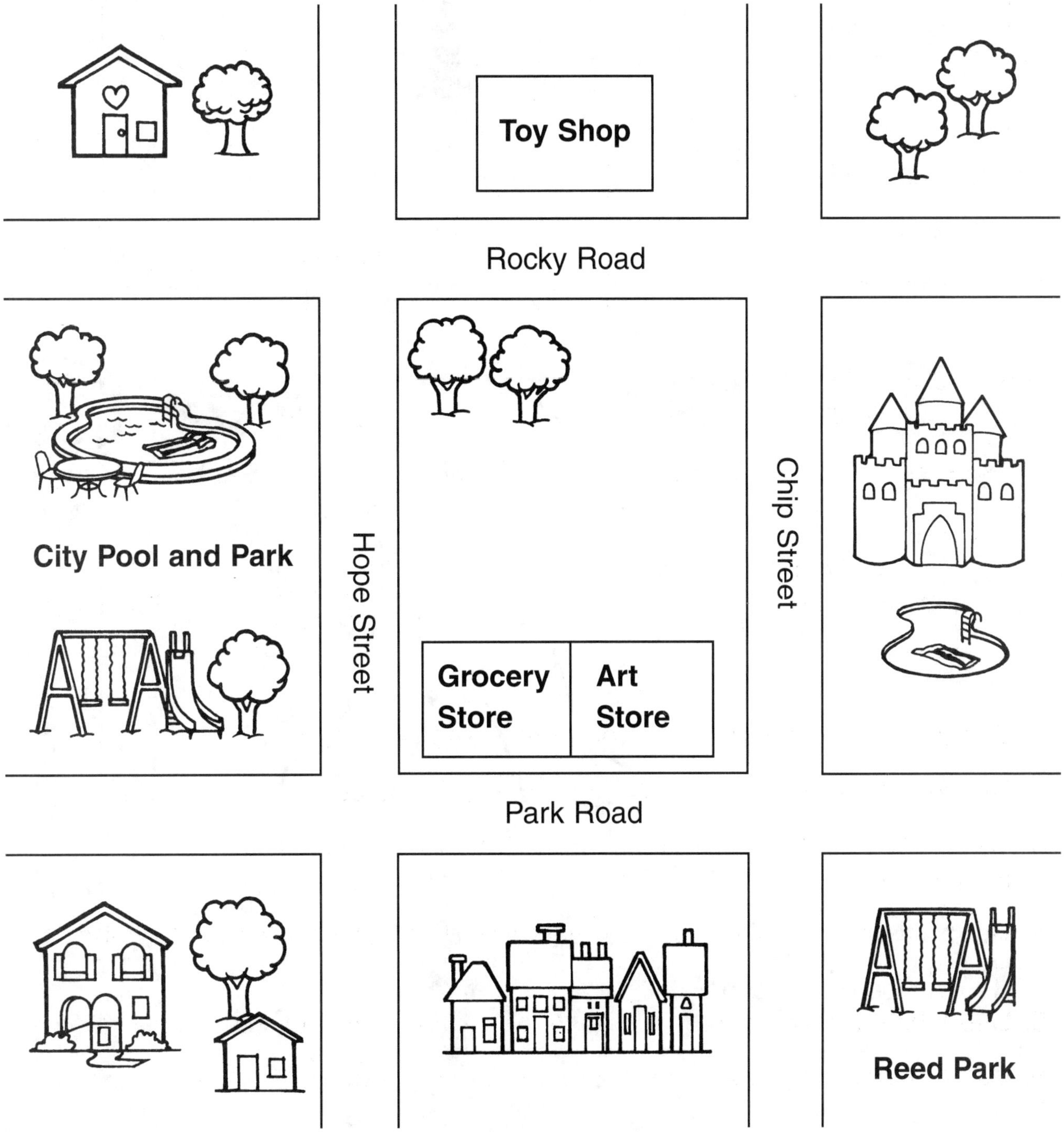

Rocky Road

City Pool and Park

Hope Street

Grocery Store

Art Store

Chip Street

Toy Shop

Park Road

Reed Park

North, South, East, and West

Color the person. Fill in the correct answer circle.

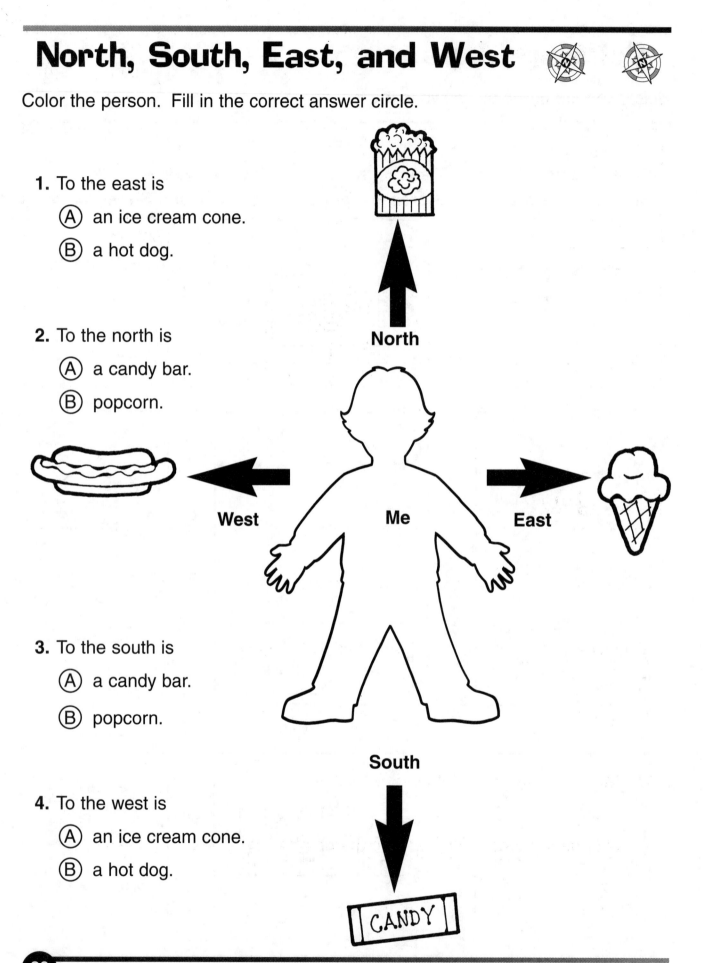

1. To the east is

   Ⓐ an ice cream cone.

   Ⓑ a hot dog.

2. To the north is

   Ⓐ a candy bar.

   Ⓑ popcorn.

3. To the south is

   Ⓐ a candy bar.

   Ⓑ popcorn.

4. To the west is

   Ⓐ an ice cream cone.

   Ⓑ a hot dog.

North

West

Me

East

South

CANDY

Old Mac's Farm

Follow the directions below.

1. Draw an 🍎 orchard to the west of the hens.

2. Draw a 🎃 patch to the north of the pig pen.

3. Draw a 🐄 pasture to the south of the sheep pasture.

4. Draw a 🚜 south of the barn.

5. Draw the farmer's 🏠 to the east of the tractor.

6. Draw a 🐦 on top of the barn.

Be a Tourist

Write the direction (**north**, **south**, **east**, or **west**) that the tourist should go to get from one site to the next.

Space Museum

The Tower

Sunny Beach

Big City

Colonial Hotel

Robot Central

The Mayflower

Frog Pond

North

West   East

South

	From ➝ To		Direction
1.			
2.			
3.			

	From ➝ To		Direction
1.			
2.			
3.			

Around the Neighborhood

Use the map to answer the questions.

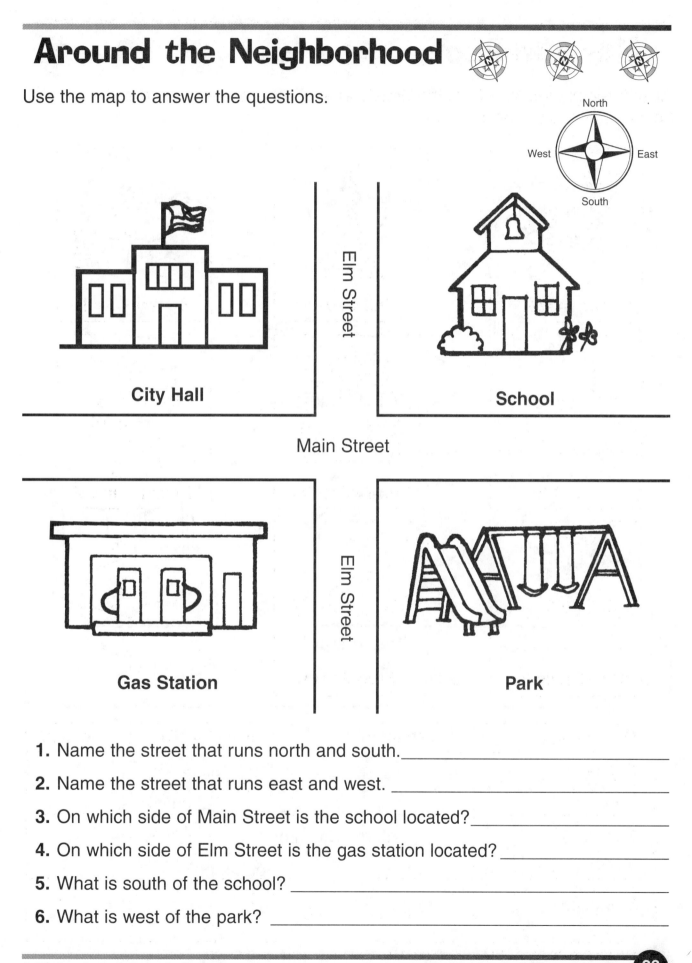

1. Name the street that runs north and south._____

2. Name the street that runs east and west. _____

3. On which side of Main Street is the school located?_____

4. On which side of Elm Street is the gas station located? _____

5. What is south of the school? _____

6. What is west of the park? _____

By the Pool

Answer each question using the Word Bank. Each answer is used only one time.

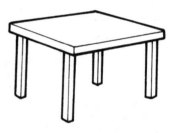

Word Bank					
east	**in**	**between**	**north**	**on top of**	**west**

1. One duck is _____ the pool.

2. The pool toys are _____ the tree and the picnic table.

3. The cat is _____ _____ _____ the swings.

4. The BBQ grill is _____ of the boom box.

5. The girl playing soccer is to the _____ of the pool.

6. The dog is _____ of the tree.

Giving Directions

Write the directions for going from one place to another. Read the directions to another person and see if the directions work!

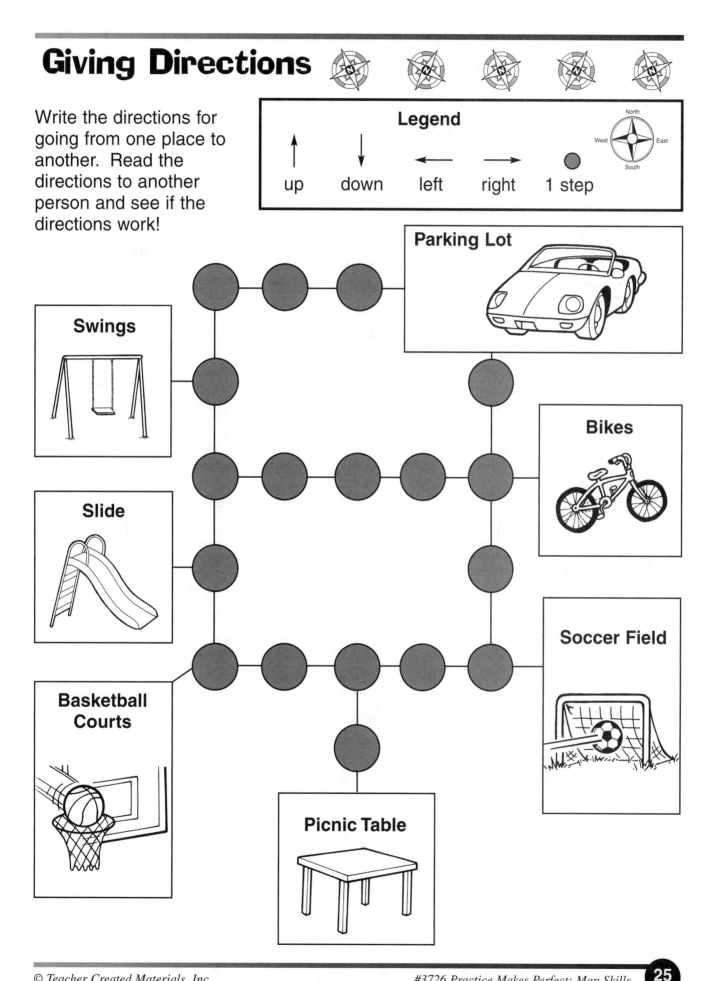

Legend

↑ up   ↓ down   ← left   → right   ● 1 step

North   West   East   South

Parking Lot

Swings

Bikes

Slide

Soccer Field

Basketball Courts

Picnic Table

Treasure Island Resort

Answer the questions below.

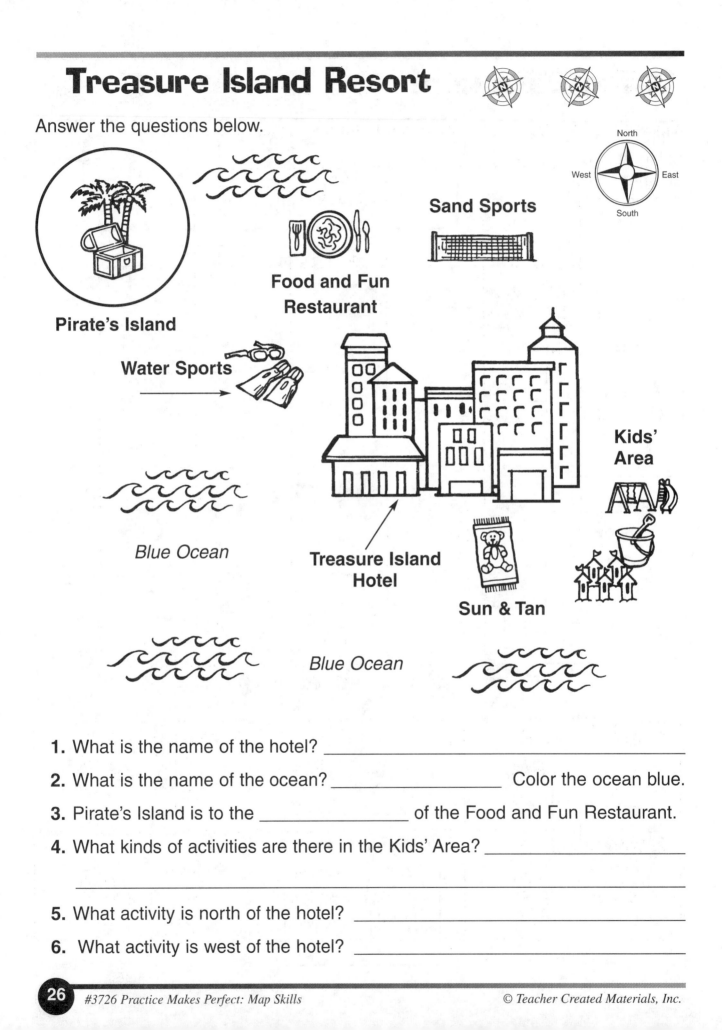

1. What is the name of the hotel? _____

2. What is the name of the ocean? _____ Color the ocean blue.

3. Pirate's Island is to the _____ of the Food and Fun Restaurant.

4. What kinds of activities are there in the Kids' Area? _____

   _____

5. What activity is north of the hotel? _____

6. What activity is west of the hotel? _____

Who's There?

Circle the character who lives at each "address" (coordinate points).

1. Who lives at B2?

2. Who lives at C5?

3. Who lives at E3?

4. Who lives at D1?

5. Who lives at A4?

6. Who lives at C1?

Where Are the Hats?

Write the coordinate points for each hat.

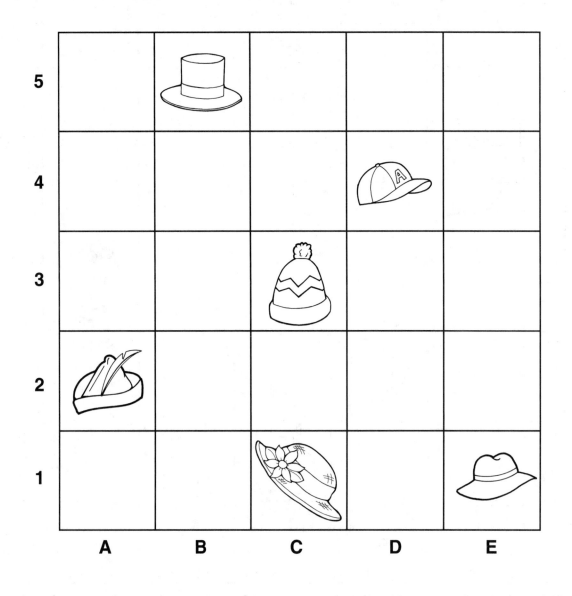

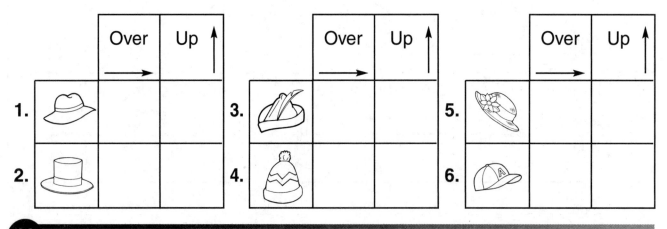

	Over →	Up ↑
1.		
2.		

	Over →	Up ↑
3.		
4.		

	Over →	Up ↑
5.		
6.		

Family Fun Park

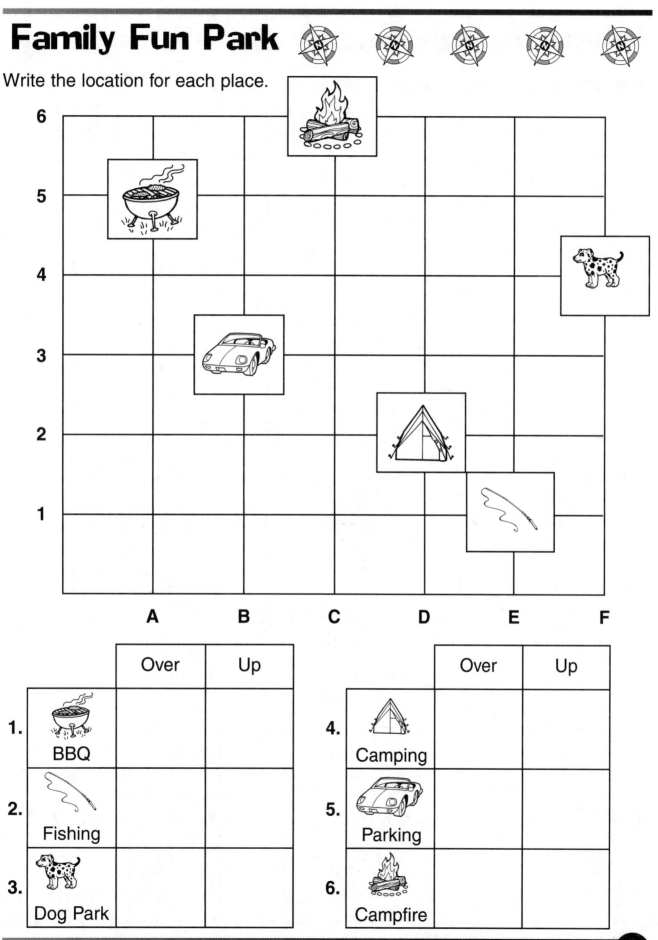

Write the location for each place.

	Over	Up
1. BBQ		
2. Fishing		
3. Dog Park		

	Over	Up
4. Camping		
5. Parking		
6. Campfire		

Find the Address

Write the address (coordinate points) for each building.

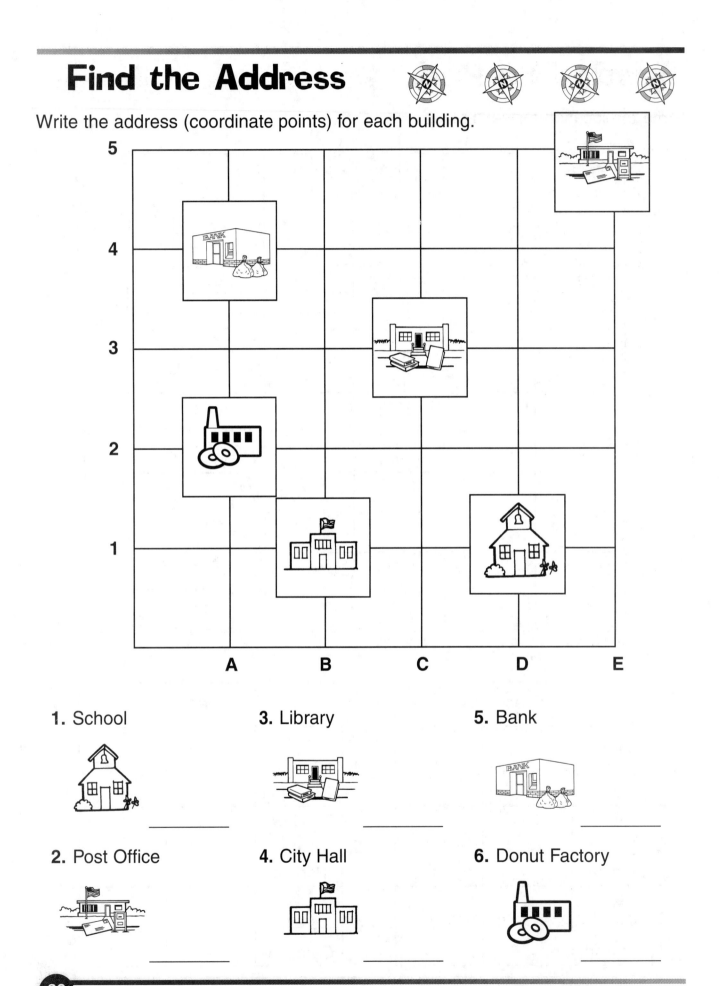

1. School

_____

2. Post Office

_____

3. Library

_____

4. City Hall

_____

5. Bank

_____

6. Donut Factory

_____

Visiting Friends

Answer each question below.

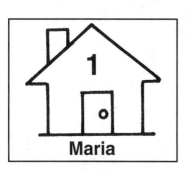 Maria

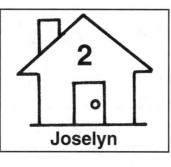 Joselyn

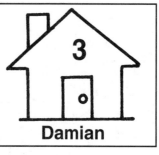 Damian

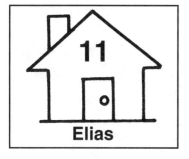 Elias

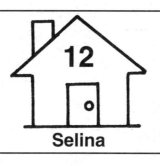 Selina

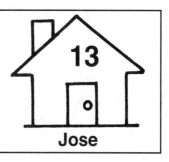 Jose

 Derikka

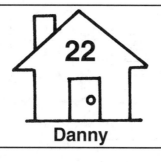 Danny

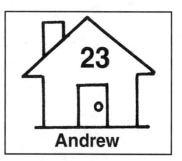 Andrew

Find out who lives in the following houses:

1. The house north of Selina's? _____

2. The house south of Elias'? _____

3. The house west of Selina's? _____

4. The house east of Joselyn's? _____

5. The house south of Damian's? _____

6. The house south of Joselyn's? _____

The School Carnival

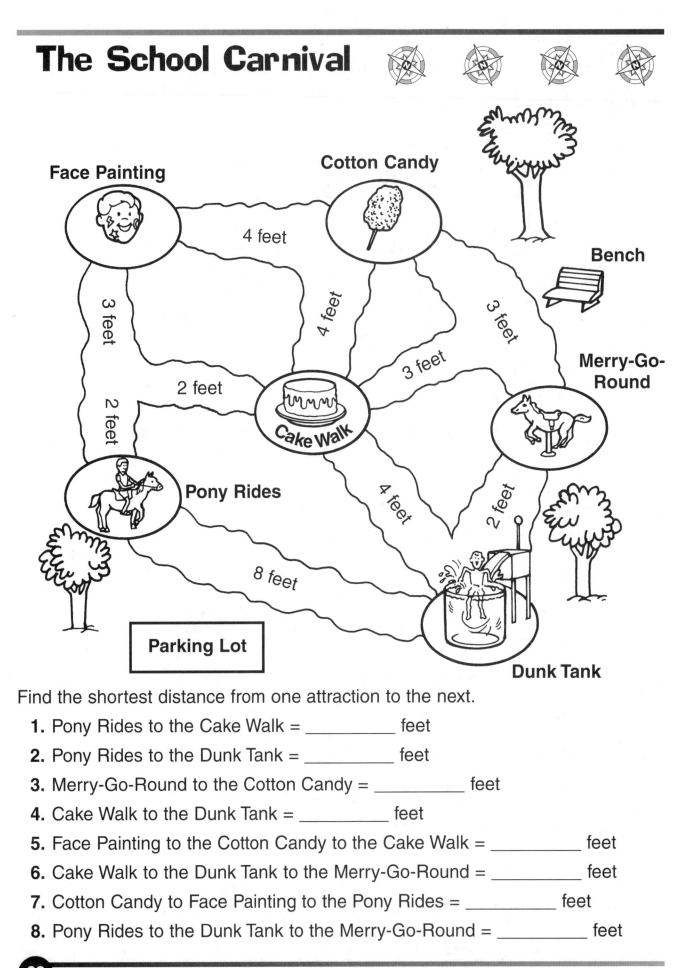

Find the shortest distance from one attraction to the next.

1. Pony Rides to the Cake Walk = _____ feet

2. Pony Rides to the Dunk Tank = _____ feet

3. Merry-Go-Round to the Cotton Candy = _____ feet

4. Cake Walk to the Dunk Tank = _____ feet

5. Face Painting to the Cotton Candy to the Cake Walk = _____ feet

6. Cake Walk to the Dunk Tank to the Merry-Go-Round = _____ feet

7. Cotton Candy to Face Painting to the Pony Rides = _____ feet

8. Pony Rides to the Dunk Tank to the Merry-Go-Round = _____ feet

Out and About

Answer the questions below.

Miniature Golf Club

A

The Park

B

Burger Time

C

E

Bowling Alley

D

Robot Factory

1. How many miles long is each road?

   A = _____ miles   B = _____ miles   C = _____ miles

   D = _____ mile   E = _____ miles

2. Write the shortest route from the Bowling Alley to Burger Time. _____
   How long is the route? _____ miles

3. Which is the shortest route to take to go from The Park to the Robot Factory? Circle one.

   Route B to E   Route A to C to D

4. Write two ways to go from the Miniature Golf Club to the Burger Time restaurant.

   Way #1 _____   Way #2 _____

   Which way is the shortest? _____

Map It Out!

Follow the directions and draw the correct symbols.

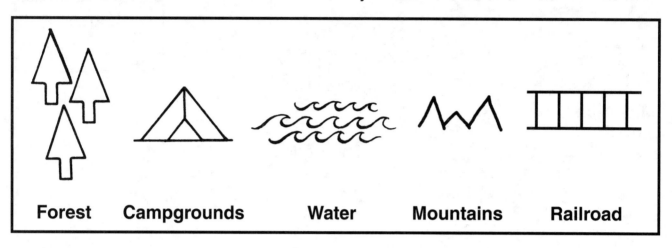

| Forest | Campgrounds | Water | Mountains | Railroad |

1. There is water in Lake Cold-as-Ice.

2. Directly east of the lake are the campgrounds.

3. Directly west of the lake is a forest.

4. South of the campgrounds is the railroad.

5. North of the lake are the mountains.

Lake Cold-as-Ice

Going Camping

Use the map to answer the questions below.

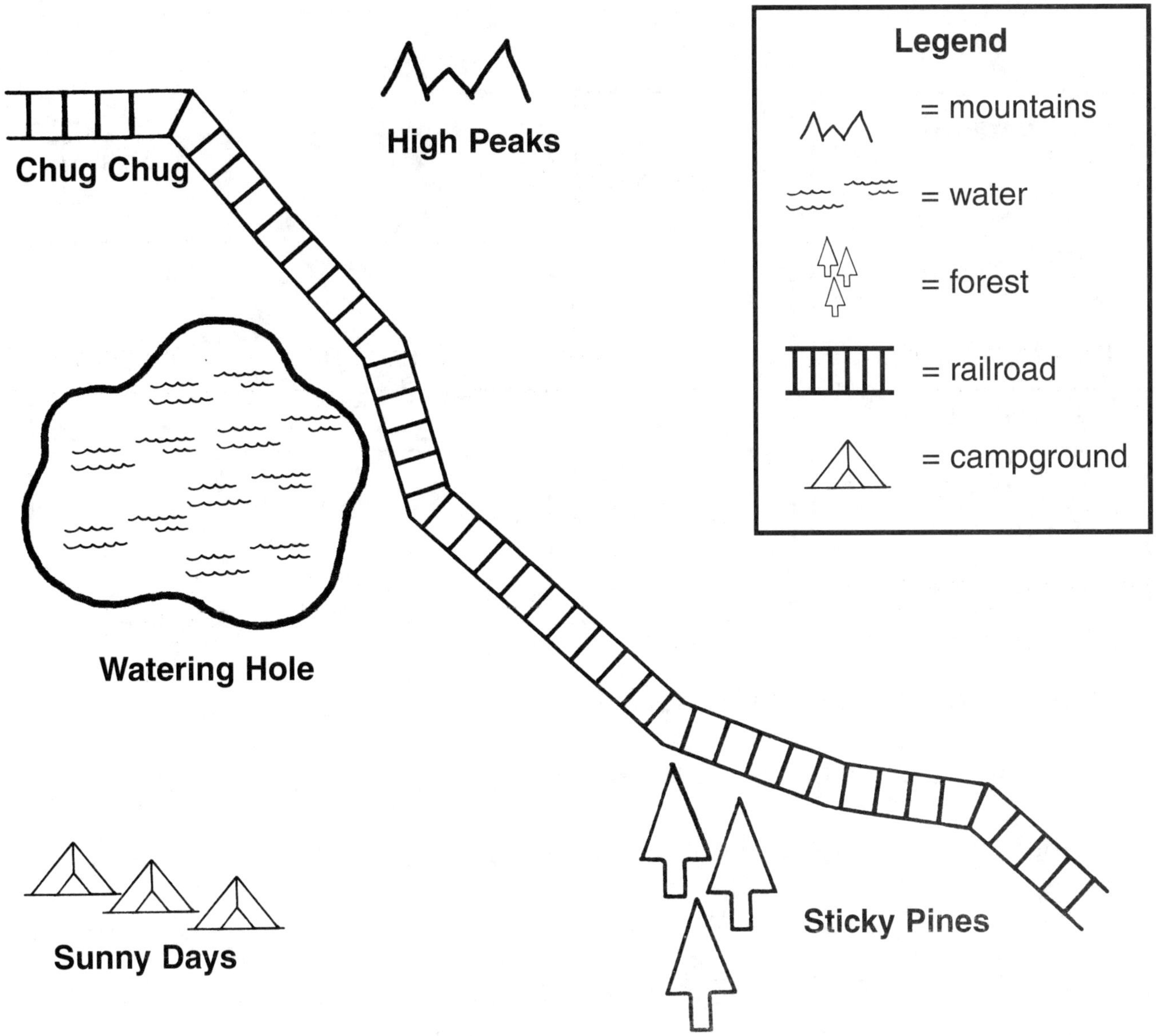

High Peaks

Chug Chug

Watering Hole

Sunny Days

Sticky Pines

Legend

ⁿ = mountains

= water

= forest

= railroad

= campground

1. What is the name of the campground? _____

2. What are the Sticky Pines ? _____

3. Where can people go fishing? _____

4. What is the name of the railroad? _____

5. What are the mountains called? _____

On the Road

Use the map and legend to answer the questions below.

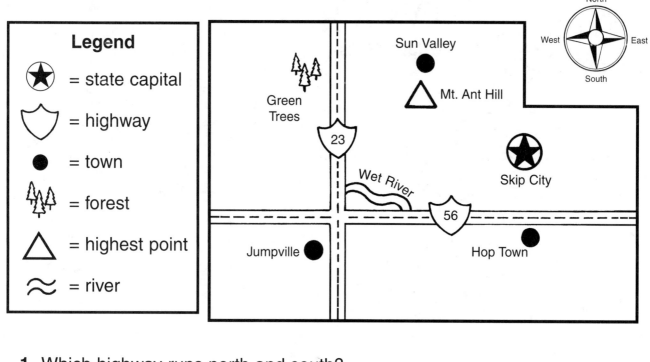

1. Which highway runs north and south? _____

2. What is the name of the state capital? _____

3. What are the names of the three towns? _____,

    _____, and _____

4. Name the town north of Mt. Ant Hill. _____

5. The forest is _____ of Highway 23.

6. Highway 56 is _____ of Jumpville.

7. Wet River runs _____ of Highway 56.

8. How many forests are shown on the map? _____

9. What town is west of Highway 23? _____

10. Which city is south of the capital? _____

At the Grocery Store

Write the aisle where each kind of food or item can be found. Use the headings to help you.

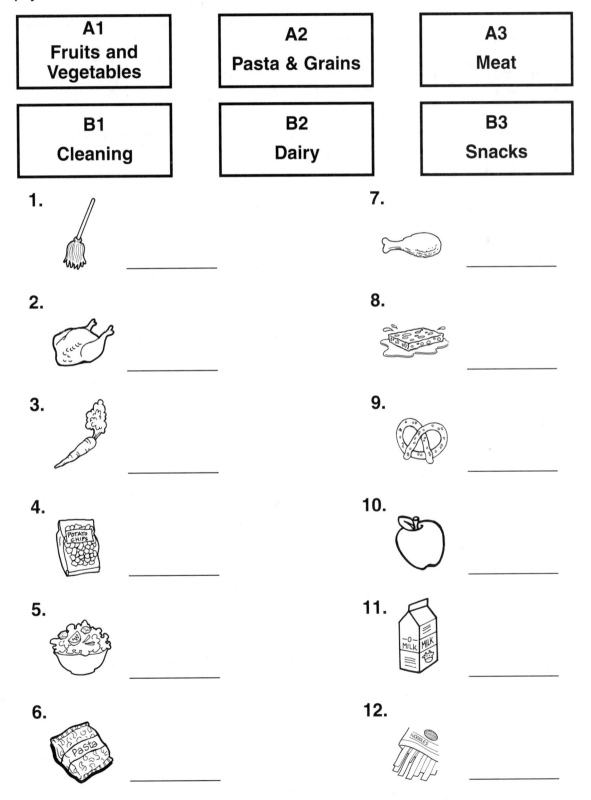

A1 Fruits and Vegetables	A2 Pasta & Grains	A3 Meat
B1 Cleaning	B2 Dairy	B3 Snacks

1. _____

2. _____

3. _____

4. _____

5. _____

6. _____

7. _____

8. _____

9. _____

10. _____

11. _____

12. _____

About the Weather

Use the weather map and legend to answer the questions below.

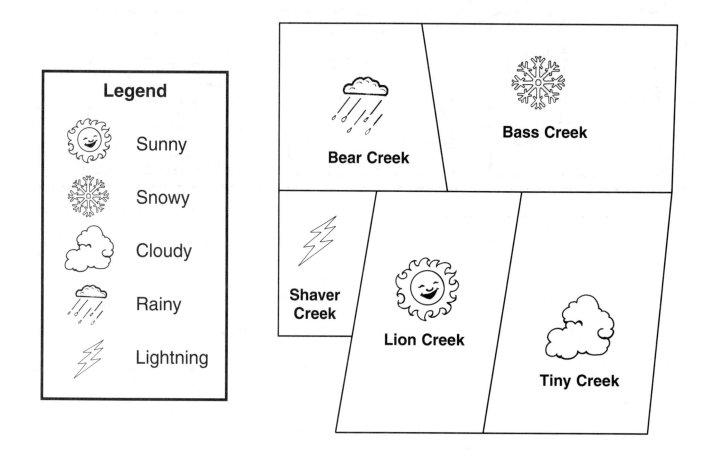

1. What was the weather like in Bass Creek? _____

2. Where was it sunny? _____

3. Where would you be able to ski? _____

4. Where was lightning seen? _____

5. What kind of weather did Tiny Creek have? _____

6. What is your favorite kind of weather? Why? _____

_____

My Classroom

Make a map of your classroom. Use the legend below to help you.

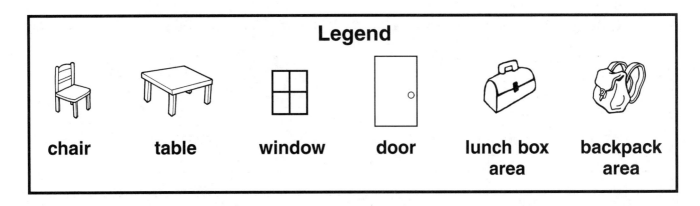

Legend

chair   table   window   door   lunch box area   backpack area

Fill in the correct answer circle.

1. The boy is _____.

(A) up   (B) down

2. The girl is _____.

(A) up   (B) down

3. The car is to the _____ of the tree.

(A) right   (B) left

4. The barn is to the _____ of the tree.

(A) right   (B) left

Mouse   **Frog**   **Cow**   **Pig**   **Cat**

5. Which animal is 3rd?

(A)   (B)   (C)

6. Which animal is 1st?

(A)   (B)   (C)

7. Which animal is to the left of the frog?

(A)   (B)   (C)

8. Which animal is to the right of the cow?

(A)   (B)   (C)

Test Practice 2

Fill in the circle next to the correct statement.

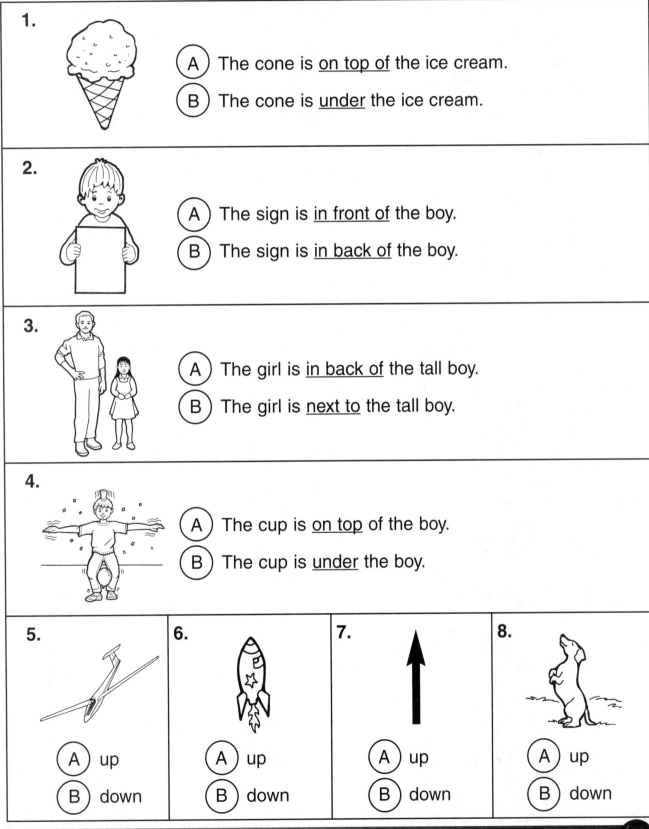

1.

(A) The cone is <u>on top of</u> the ice cream.

(B) The cone is <u>under</u> the ice cream.

2.

(A) The sign is <u>in front of</u> the boy.

(B) The sign is <u>in back of</u> the boy.

3.

(A) The girl is <u>in back of</u> the tall boy.

(B) The girl is <u>next to</u> the tall boy.

4.

(A) The cup is <u>on top</u> of the boy.

(B) The cup is <u>under</u> the boy.

5.

(A) up

(B) down

6.

(A) up

(B) down

7.

(A) up

(B) down

8.

(A) up

(B) down

Test Practice 3

Use the maps to fill in the correct answer circles.

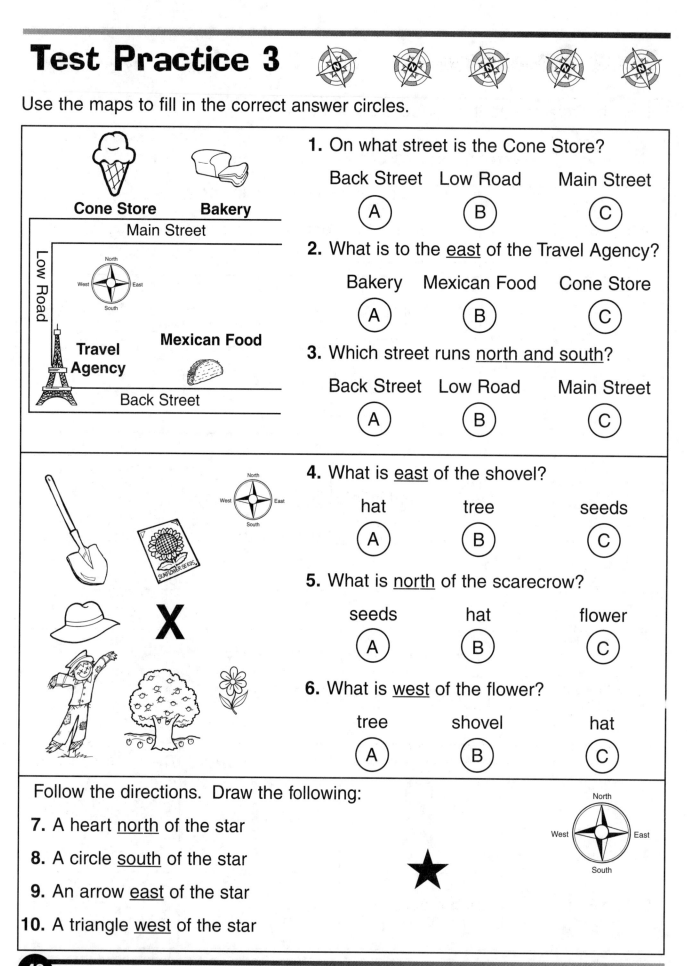

1. On what street is the Cone Store?

Back Street — (A) Low Road — (B) Main Street — (C)

2. What is to the <u>east</u> of the Travel Agency?

Bakery — (A) Mexican Food — (B) Cone Store — (C)

3. Which street runs <u>north and south</u>?

Back Street — (A) Low Road — (B) Main Street — (C)

4. What is <u>east</u> of the shovel?

hat — (A) tree — (B) seeds — (C)

5. What is <u>north</u> of the scarecrow?

seeds — (A) hat — (B) flower — (C)

6. What is <u>west</u> of the flower?

tree — (A) shovel — (B) hat — (C)

Follow the directions. Draw the following:

7. A heart <u>north</u> of the star

8. A circle <u>south</u> of the star

9. An arrow <u>east</u> of the star

10. A triangle <u>west</u> of the star

Test Practice 4

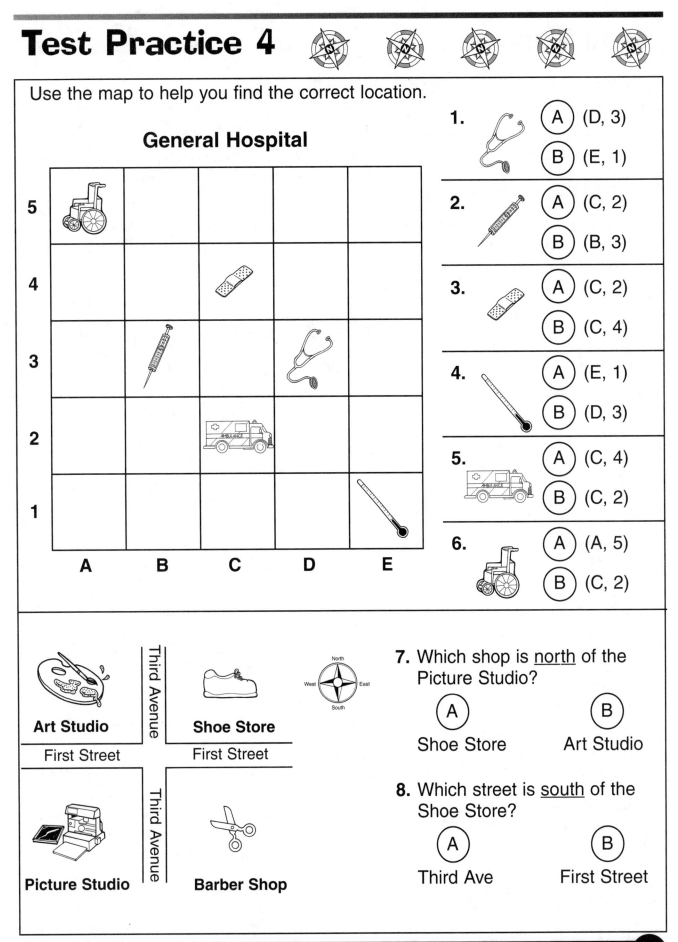

Use the map to help you find the correct location.

General Hospital

1. Ⓐ (D, 3)   Ⓑ (E, 1)

2. Ⓐ (C, 2)   Ⓑ (B, 3)

3. Ⓐ (C, 2)   Ⓑ (C, 4)

4. Ⓐ (E, 1)   Ⓑ (D, 3)

5. Ⓐ (C, 4)   Ⓑ (C, 2)

6. Ⓐ (A, 5)   Ⓑ (C, 2)

Art Studio

Third Avenue

Shoe Store

First Street   First Street

North
West   East
South

Third Avenue

Picture Studio   Barber Shop

7. Which shop is <u>north</u> of the Picture Studio?

Ⓐ Shoe Store   Ⓑ Art Studio

8. Which street is <u>south</u> of the Shoe Store?

Ⓐ Third Ave   Ⓑ First Street

Test Practice 5

Use the map to fill in the correct answer circle.

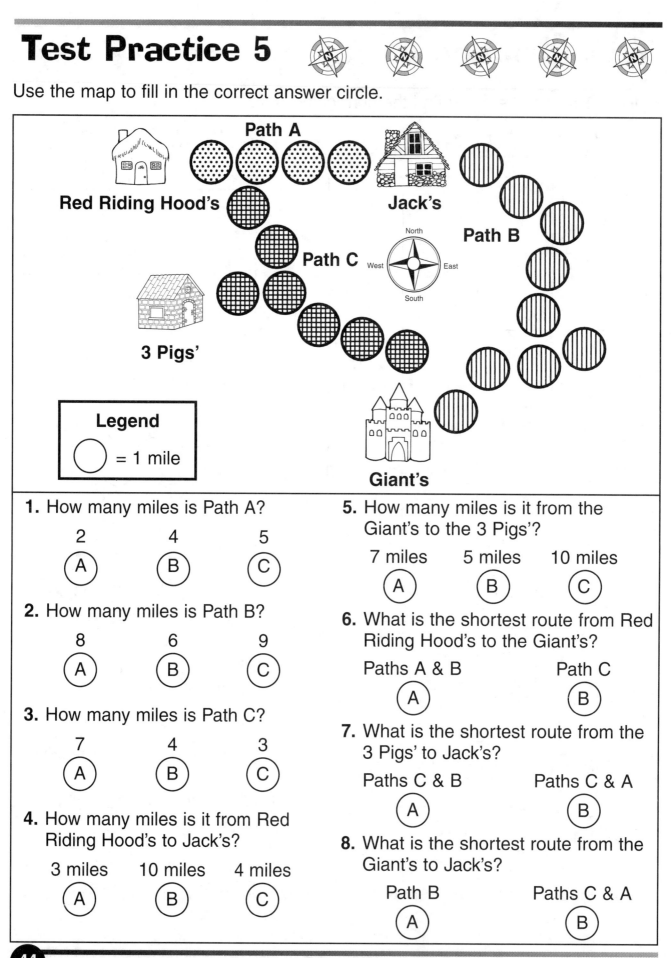

Legend

◯ = 1 mile

1. How many miles is Path A?

   2   4   5

   (A)   (B)   (C)

2. How many miles is Path B?

   8   6   9

   (A)   (B)   (C)

3. How many miles is Path C?

   7   4   3

   (A)   (B)   (C)

4. How many miles is it from Red Riding Hood's to Jack's?

   3 miles   10 miles   4 miles

   (A)   (B)   (C)

5. How many miles is it from the Giant's to the 3 Pigs'?

   7 miles   5 miles   10 miles

   (A)   (B)   (C)

6. What is the shortest route from Red Riding Hood's to the Giant's?

   Paths A & B   Path C

   (A)   (B)

7. What is the shortest route from the 3 Pigs' to Jack's?

   Paths C & B   Paths C & A

   (A)   (B)

8. What is the shortest route from the Giant's to Jack's?

   Path B   Paths C & A

   (A)   (B)

#3726 Practice Makes Perfect: Map Skills

Test Practice 6

Use the map and the legend to fill in the correct answer circle.

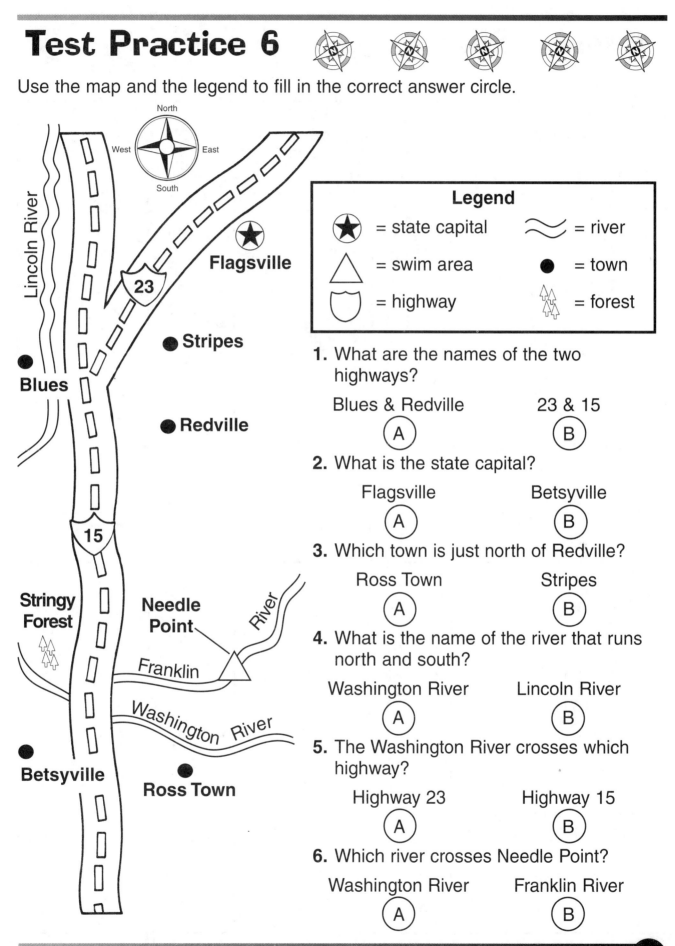

Legend

⭐ = state capital   ∼ = river

△ = swim area   ● = town

⛨ = highway   🌲 = forest

1. What are the names of the two highways?

Blues & Redville   23 & 15

(A)   (B)

2. What is the state capital?

Flagsville   Betsyville

(A)   (B)

3. Which town is just north of Redville?

Ross Town   Stripes

(A)   (B)

4. What is the name of the river that runs north and south?

Washington River   Lincoln River

(A)   (B)

5. The Washington River crosses which highway?

Highway 23   Highway 15

(A)   (B)

6. Which river crosses Needle Point?

Washington River   Franklin River

(A)   (B)

Answer Sheet

Test Practice 1 **Page 40**	**Test Practice 2** **Page 41**	**Test Practice 3** **Page 42**
1. Ⓐ Ⓑ	1. Ⓐ Ⓑ	1. Ⓐ Ⓑ Ⓒ
2. Ⓐ Ⓑ	2. Ⓐ Ⓑ	2. Ⓐ Ⓑ Ⓒ
3. Ⓐ Ⓑ	3. Ⓐ Ⓑ	3. Ⓐ Ⓑ Ⓒ
4. Ⓐ Ⓑ	4. Ⓐ Ⓑ	4. Ⓐ Ⓑ Ⓒ
5. Ⓐ Ⓑ Ⓒ	5. Ⓐ Ⓑ	5. Ⓐ Ⓑ Ⓒ
6. Ⓐ Ⓑ Ⓒ	6. Ⓐ Ⓑ	6. Ⓐ Ⓑ Ⓒ
7. Ⓐ Ⓑ Ⓒ	7. Ⓐ Ⓑ	7.–10.
8. Ⓐ Ⓑ Ⓒ	8. Ⓐ Ⓑ	★

Test Practice 4 **Page 43**	**Test Practice 5** **Page 44**	**Test Practice 6** **Page 45**
1. Ⓐ Ⓑ	1. Ⓐ Ⓑ Ⓒ	1. Ⓐ Ⓑ
2. Ⓐ Ⓑ	2. Ⓐ Ⓑ Ⓒ	2. Ⓐ Ⓑ
3. Ⓐ Ⓑ	3. Ⓐ Ⓑ Ⓒ	3. Ⓐ Ⓑ
4. Ⓐ Ⓑ	4. Ⓐ Ⓑ Ⓒ	4. Ⓐ Ⓑ
5. Ⓐ Ⓑ	5. Ⓐ Ⓑ Ⓒ	5. Ⓐ Ⓑ
6. Ⓐ Ⓑ	6. Ⓐ Ⓑ	6. Ⓐ Ⓑ
7. Ⓐ Ⓑ	7. Ⓐ Ⓑ	
8. Ⓐ Ⓑ	8. Ⓐ Ⓑ	

Answer Key

Page 4
1. D
2. G
3. H
4. E
5. B
6. F
7. C
8. A

Page 5
1. up
2. down
3. up
4. up
5. down

Page 6
1. left
2. right
3. right
4. left

Page 7
1. right
2. left
3. right
4. left
5. left

Page 8
1. 3
2. 6
3. 1st
4. 2nd
5. 6
6. 3rd
7. 5
8. The Cooks

Page 9
Ordinals going from top to bottom: 5th, 4th, 3rd, 2nd, 1st
1. 5
2. 5
3. Granny

4. Cat
5. 4th
6. 3rd
7. Baby
8. Teacher
9. Cat
10. 4

Page 10
1. horse
2. train
3. bus
4. bike
5. plane
6. boat
7. train

Page 11
1. 2nd on the right
2. 4th on the right
3. 1st on the left
4. 1st on the right
5. 2nd on the left
6. 3rd on the left
7. 4th on the left
8. 3rd on the right

Page 12
Check to make sure items are in their correct positions.

Page 13
1. inside
2. outside
3. outside
4. inside
5. outside
6. inside

Page 14
1. on top of
2. behind
3. next to
4. under
5. in front of

Page 15
1. next to
2. between
3. the right of
4. the left of
5. beside

Page 16
1. up
2. below/under
3. under/below
4. above/over
5. over/above
6. down

Page 17
1. on top of
2. on
3. behind
4. in front of
5. under
6. inside
7. right of
8. next to
9. outside

Page 18
1. Go right to the end of the path and then go up.
2. Go down on the diagonal path.
3. Go up and then right till the end of the path. Then go down.
4. Go down and then to the right. At the first cross street, go down till the end and then go right. At the first cross street, go down to Baseball Uniforms.
5. Go down and turn left at the first cross street. Go

down at the next cross street to Baseball Uniforms.
6. Go down to the end of the path and turn left to Shoes.

Page 19
Check to make sure each item is colored correctly.

Page 20
1. A.
2. B.
3. A.
4. B.

Page 21
Reading from left to right
1. Top row: apple orchard
2. Middle row: pumpkin patch, bird on the barn, cow pasture
3. Bottom row: tractor, farmer's house

Page 22
1. south
2. east
3. west
4. north
5. west
6. south

Page 23
1. Elm Street
2. Main Street
3. north
4. west
5. park
6. gas station

Answer Key

Page 24
1. in
2. between
3. on top of
4. north
5. west
6. east

Page 25
Directions will vary.

Page 26
1. Treasure Island Hotel
2. Blue Ocean
3. west
4. swings and a slide, playing in the sand, building sand castles
5. Sand Sports
6. Water Sports

Page 27
1. girl with long hair
2. girl with braid
3. boy with dark, curly hair
4. boy with spiked hair
5. boy with freckles
6. girl with short hair

Page 28
1. E, 1
2. B, 5
3. A, 2
4. C, 3
5. C, 1
6. D, 4

Page 29
1. A, 5
2. E, 1
3. F, 4
4. D, 2
5. B, 3
6. C, 6

Page 30
1. D, 1
2. E, 5
3. C, 3
4. B, 1
5. A, 4
6. A, 2

Page 31
1. Joselyn
2. Derikka
3. Elias
4. Damian
5. Jose
6. Selina

Page 32
1. 4 feet
2. 8 feet
3. 3 feet
4. 4 feet
5. 8 feet
6. 6 feet
7. 9 feet
8. 10 feet

Page 33
1. A = 3, B = 4, C = 2, D = 1, E = 6
2. D to E, 7 miles
3. Route A to C to D
4. A to B or C to D to E, A to B is the shortest route.

Page 34
Check the placement of symbols to make sure the directions were followed.

Page 35
1. Sunny Days
2. Forest
3. Watering Hole
4. Chug Chug
5. High Peaks

Page 36
1. Highway 23
2. Skip City
3. Sun Valley, Jumpville, Hop Town
4. Sun Valley
5. west
6. north
7. north
8. 1
9. Jumpville
10. Hop Town

Page 37
1. B1
2. A3
3. A1
4. B3
5. A1
6. A2
7. A3
8. B1
9. B3
10. A1
11. B2
12. A2

Page 38
1. snowy
2. Lion Creek
3. Bass Creek
4. Shaver Creek
5. cloudy
6. Answers will vary.

Page 39
Check maps for correct placement of items.

Page 40
1. B
2. A
3. B
4. A
5. A

6. B
7. C
8. A

Page 41
1. B
2. A
3. B
4. A
5. B
6. A
7. A
8. A

Page 42
1. C
2. B
3. B
4. C
5. B
6. A
7.–10.

Page 43
1. A
2. B
3. B
4. A

5. B
6. A
7. B
8. B

Page 44
1. B
2. C
3. A
4. C

5. B
6. B
7. B
8. A

Page 45
1. B
2. A
3. B

4. B
5. B
6. B